WE WANT TO OBEY

OBEYING

DOING, doing—I'm always doing!
   And I want to obey,
Because God's Book says, "Children, obey—
   Do what Mommy and Daddy say."

Our parents love and help us
   So very much each day;
Shouldn't we be happy
   To do just what they say?

Mommy and Daddy say, "When you wake up, play quietly until the clock rings."

WAKING

Most *babies* are like alarm clocks!
   They make noise when they're through sleeping;
But *I'm* awake, and you can see
   How very still I'm keeping!

When Mommy and Daddy are sleeping,
 We play so we won't miss them,
But when the clock rings, ting-a-ling!
 We jump right up and kiss them!

. . .

It's a good day when we obey—
 God's Book tells us so!

Mommy says,
"Wash your face and hands
and come to breakfast."

WASHING UP

Soap and water are great fun
  If we're blowing bubbles,
But when we splash while washing up,
  We have mop-up troubles!

But if we play instead of wash,
  Mom calls, "Please do hurry."
When we're careful to obey,
  Mommy does not worry!

It's a good day when we obey—
  God's Book tells us so!

Daddy says,
"Let's bow our heads and close our eyes
and thank God for our food."

GIVING THANKS FOR FOOD

We thank You, Lord, for Your great love,
   We thank You for this food,
We pray that it will make us strong
   To do what's right and good.
     In Jesus' name, Amen.

Mommy says,
"Eat your food now. And let's
try to have good table manners."

EATING

Where's the bunny?
    There's a bunny at the bottom of my plate.
There's the bunny!
    See, he's smiling at the lot of food I ate!

WORSHIPING GOD TOGETHER

Daddy says,
"Let's be quiet now.
It's time for our
family worship."

After breakfast, in our house,
    Is Bible-reading time;
My Daddy opens up God's Book,
    And on his knees I climb.

Then, while I snuggle close to him,
    And Mommy listens, too,
My Daddy reads to us the things
    That God wants us to do—
To help as little Samuel did;
    Obey like David, brave;
And to love Jesus, God's own Son,
    The Saviour that He gave.

I like to hear my Daddy's voice;
   I don't know all he's saying,
But Mommy explains it some to me,
   And then we kneel for praying.

After we have talked to God,
   I like to say, "Amen!"
Daddy's proud of me and lifts me
   Up to the ceiling then!

Mommy says,
"Time to finish dressing now!"

PUTTING ON MY SHOES

I like to dress all by myself,
    And I can be quite neat;
But when my shoes go different ways,
    I know they're on "wrong feet"!

So then I change them—and I even
    Try to do my laces;
It's getting easy for me now
    To poke them in right places!

Mommy says,
"Please hold your head still."

COMBING MY HAIR

When Mommy combs my curly hair,
   I try to hold quite still;
If I twist and squirm, it pulls—
   Every time it will!

Yes, it's always ouch, ouch, ouch!
   When I twist and disobey;
But the quieter I am,
   The sooner I can play!

It's a good day when I obey—
   God's Book tells me so!

PLAYING

Mommy says,
"Now you may
run along and play."

Boys like to play "fix-it" like Dad;
   They like toy trucks and balls.
They think it's fun to be a fireman
   Or a trucker on long hauls!

Girls like to play "dress-up" like Mom;
   They like tea sets and dolls.
What fun to "entertain" their friends,
   Or make long telephone calls!

When Mommy calls, "Brother, Sister, come!"
   We still would like to play—
But God's Book says, "Children, obey—
   Do what Mommy and Daddy say."

And so we quickly put away
  Our trucks and dolls and balls;
We really have a better time
  If we come when Mother calls!

Sometimes Mommy needs our help;
Sometimes she smiles, "Surprise!"
Whichever, aren't you glad to see
The love shine in her eyes?

At last Mommy and Daddy say, "It's bedtime— time to sleep."

OBEYING AT SLEEPY TIME

Doing, doing—we're always doing—
   Busy at work or play!
But aren't you glad for rest and sleep
   At the end of day?

See—Sister and her Raggedy Ann,
   They are quick to obey;
But will Brother leave his color book?
   Will he come right away?

What do *you* think?
 Yes, he will, I know;
IT'S A GOOD DAY WHEN WE OBEY—
 GOD'S BOOK TELLS US SO!

The Port Town Publishing
Tiny Doings Books
is a wonderful collection written
by Ruth McNaughton Hinds.
This series of books
is for Pre-schoolers, giving
them a solid, basic conception
of God's love, His creation,
and conduct that pleases God.

ISBN 1-59466-056-5

$7.95